Soul, Inc.

A Copywriter's Guide to Creating Meaningful and Memorable Brand Identities

by Michael Phillips

Soul, Inc.
A Copywriter's Guide to Creating
Meaningful and Memorable Brand Identities

 Published 2025.
Printed in the United States of America
34 33 32 31 30 29 28 27 26 25   1 2 3 4 5

ISBN (Print): 978-1-887229-66-1
ISBN (ebook): 978-1-887229-67-8

Published by First Flight Books
firstflightbooks.net

Design by One Design Company

Contents

Where Am I?

Advertising is grotesque and unrecognizable. It used to be that if you wrote a single line of powerful copy, you could sell a product and call it a job well done. You could spend hours, days, or weeks (or fifteen seconds in the shower) coming up with that line, and you would get paid handsomely for it. You could write two hundred words in an ad and, if it was interesting, people would read it.

Then came Google and "search." Every paragraph of copy now needed to have keywords, even if it completely destroyed the poetry of the narrative. Even if it made the copy nearly nonsensical. I imagine trained copy editors fled the advertising industry en masse.

Then came "storytelling." Every account manager started asking, "Where is the story? We need a story. But don't forget to put in a bunch of keywords for Google." Suddenly, every ad was a story. Even the short ones. Every television ad became some sort of vignette (and it continues). You have to suffer through some kind of meaningless trope before you even realize what the product is or how it will make some part of your life just a little bit better. If you ever do. As a writer, of course I love reading and writing a good story. But not when they are hollow vehicles intended to sell you on a new phone plan.

Then came social media and influencers. A plague, if you ask me. An imaginary reality making you feel inferior so that you'll buy whatever it is that they swear makes them the most popular people on the planet. Every strategy came down to finding an influencer to make vignettes for us. "Hey, guys... you HAVE to see this really amazing face tenderizer. You have GOT to try it. OK, here's a story about it and how awesome I am!" I'm glad their "influence" is rapidly declining.

Now we have AI. If you think AI won't threaten your job, you are wrong. Agencies and even clients have quickly caught on to the fact that AI can do most copywriting jobs with a few simple prompts. Sure, it might start to all sound the same after a while, but these days, it's a game of quantity over quality.

I'm probably skipping over a bunch of other transgressions that have chipped away at the temple of copywriting. But my point is that the art and business of copywriting has been under siege for some time now. And it still is.

If, like me, you came into copywriting expecting glorious late nights pecking away at your laptop with a glass of really good bourbon at your side until the perfect line of copy poured out of your fingertips, you might be asking yourself, Where the hell am I?

Unfortunately, in a way, we've dug our own hole. Copywriters give Google something to work with. Copywriters are the ones who make a story something that can actually sell a product. Copywriters are who gave the ideas to every schmuck and narcissistic peacock with an iPhone and a rented poolside cabana. Without copywriters, AI would return a mouth full of marbles when you asked it for a snappy headline. But I digress.

Before you get the idea that I'm some fossil who used to work on Madison Avenue, I am not. I kind of wish I were. I entered advertising and marketing much later than that, but still, in my early days, we copywriters were still writing great copy. Copy that hit hard. Copy that sold a product. Then all of this other stuff happened. It was not what I expected when I was preparing for my first advertising job by reading David Ogilvy's Ogilvy on Advertising. But I've always been a fake-it-'til-you-make-it guy, one who always looked out for what could kill me next. So I was quick to understand that the golden age of advertising was dead, and that things were going to get unwieldy. Somewhere in there I recognized that the real power resided in the brand. And for copywriters specifically, in authoring the brand.

Advertising and marketing might be a bastardized cesspool of unpredictability at the moment, but there is no one better equipped to shape the future of advertising and marketing than you.

Through the brand.

The Almighty Copywriter

The copywriter is the most important and influential role in marketing and advertising. That's because they are responsible for the message, and that is what drives every other activity in the industry. Logo design, color palettes, typography, content strategy, advertising, social media—it's all driven by the message. While design and marketing are vital to advancing the message, it is the copywriter who bestows the brand its identity and, therefore, sets its course.

Brands typically get one shot at launching an identity. Once it's out there in the world, it must form an immediate connection. It needs to stand out, and it needs to stick for a very, very long time. The more meaningful the brand identity, the higher the chances are that the brand has a long and profitable life. We, as consumers, like to try new brands. But we invest in brands that we feel connected to. These are the brands that last. These are the brands with soul.

If the brand fails to make a connection, it is a massive loss. Most likely the brand will fail before ever having the chance to rebuild its identity. The business might rebuild, but the brand is likely dead. It is a costly misfire.

And the single biggest reason for failure is a weak message.

The single most important reason brands are successful is a powerful message. The message, in all its forms, begins with the Verbal Brand Identity.

> **"**
>
> **The single most important reason brands are successful is a powerful message.**

Congratulations. You have one of the most exciting jobs in the field. And an immense responsibility.

My name is Mike Phillips. I started my career in journalism, before moving to the dark side: Advertising. I mention this because I believe that my modest and brief foray into journalism built an invaluable foundation for the work of a copywriter. Specifically, these three tenets that I was taught to be a solid journalist:

1. **Dig for the truth**
2. **Validate that truth**
3. **Tell it in a moving way**

In this book, I will take you through my process of creating soulful brands with powerful and memorable verbal brand identities. While I've been a writer in one form or another for about twenty years, I don't claim to be a guru. This is simply what I have learned and practiced on my way to what has been a very successful and varied career thus far. I did not go to school for marketing, advertising, or journalism. I'm not highly educated; I have just your standard bachelor of arts degree in an unrelated major. I've had some great mentors along the way, and I just dove into the work.

That work has included naming brands; writing their stories; developing their personalities; writing their taglines, headlines, and website copy; creating their advertising; creating pitch decks; writing video scripts and social media content; and ghost writing articles.

All of it starts with the verbal brand identity. It is the most essential part of any brand, and the longest lasting. And there is just one thing that every modern brand identity must do to be successful:
It must have soul.

There are many different ways to create a verbal brand identity. Google it. You'll find yourself bouncing all over the place in no time. You'll also find a lot of the same. The approach I take is similar and different to much of what you might find, with the biggest differences being the order in which I do things; the ways that I approach and get to know brands; and the fact that I don't think about the consumer much, and competitors hardly at all.

You and I were put on this earth to write stories. And I don't know many truly great stories that were written with a target audience in mind. I believe that the best brands are the ones that believe in themselves, their vision, and their mission. Those are brands with soul.

In this book you will learn what you need to know to build modern, memorable, and unique brand identities. In some places you will find step-by-step guides, and in other places I'll point you in the general direction. You're a writer. You don't need me to tell you how to write. Anyway, the best brand identities have a piece of the writer in them. What I hope to provide is some grist for the mill, and a few pointers along the way.

I hope you enjoy the book. And I would be very proud to know if it helped you create something meaningful for you and for your clients.

A Note About AI

The rise of AI in the advertising industry has raised many questions, ranging from "Will it take my job?" to "How much should I use it?" When it comes to creating brand identities, I believe the answer to the first question is "no." Because AI pulls information from what already exists in the world, and we are creating something new, it will be a long time before we can just hit a button and get a meaningful brand identity. I have used AI extensively, and I can tell you that if it is lacking one thing, it is soul.

The answer to the second question is a bit more nuanced. I believe that AI can be incredibly useful for copywriters. I use AI in two primary ways:

1. **As a research assistant.** If I need quick answers, AI is a great resource. I might ask for lists of competitors, industry overviews, audience profile info, or any other noncritical and noncreative output. But use caution, and fact check. Don't just take AI's word for it. It makes mistakes.

2. **As a junior copywriter.** If I'm stuck on something or need a little nudge to get the ideas rolling, I'll use AI to write headlines and copy, to explore tone, or to write quick sample narratives. The usual result is that I'll find a little inspiration to get me moving in the right direction, even if it's just a few words.

The key to success with AI is to provide the tool with a great brief. Just like you would if kicking off a project for a team, prescribe the outcome that you want; provide clear guardrails; and leave a little latitude for sideways "thinking."

Use AI as much as you want. But use it like the drunk uses the lamppost: for support, not illumination.

Purpose, Value, Personality: The Trifecta of a Soulful Brand Identity

What is a soulful brand? And why does it matter if a brand has soul?

Soulful brands speak to the consumer on a personal level. They go beyond the utility of their products and services to form a connection with people. If you think about any of the brands that you value most, and that you might even advocate for, the chances are good that you feel some kind of bond with those brands. They do more for you than provide a product at a fair price.

You might wear Levi's jeans not just because they are comfortable and priced well, but because you feel that they are representative of your ideals as a youthful, hard-working, down-to-earth person. You might fly Southwest Airlines because of its friendly and democratic nature, which reflects your own. Or you might buy Burt's Bees lip balm because of its natural, homegrown ethos. All of these companies offer the same or very similar products and services as dozens of competitors, who might even offer higher quality. Yet these brands succeed because they have established deep connections with their audiences. They have soul.

> **Today's consumers need a personal, existential reason to choose your brand over another.**

Never before has it been easier to start a business. With modern tools and platforms, the barrier to entry is very low. I started my agency in under a week with a few apps and a laptop. Even more complex industries have become easier and more affordable to enter with the rapid rise of automation. Established brands are reaping the rewards too, with the ability to expand into new sectors quickly with lower risk. This means that the arena has become far more crowded, and consumers have more choices than ever. Standing out from the crowd and maintaining customer loyalty—that is, making a connection with people—is where many battles are won and lost in the modern business era.

Today's consumers have proven time and again that they prefer to buy from brands that they can identify with. They need a personal, existential reason to choose your brand over another.

We can create this by articulating **Purpose**, **Value**, and **Personality**.

- **Purpose** (clearly and quickly communicating the brand's mission and, later, what it does)
- **Value** (defining what tangible and intangible or emotional benefits the brand offers the consumer)
- **Personality** (humanizing the brand with a natural voice)

By creating meaningful brands with soul, we are setting up our clients to be more successful and more profitable. And that is what we are here to do.

But before we get into all that, let's evaluate the playing field.

The Client Is Not the Devil

It took me a good ten years to understand that the Client is not a necessary evil. Rather, they are vital to producing the best work of your life.

Before that? I resented just about every client I'd ever had. Not because they were bad people (one or two were) but because I felt like they always got in the way of my great ideas. This is not the case.

As copywriters, our job is to breathe life into a vision. It is not to come up with pretty words to restate what someone else has already written. That is a very important distinction. We are not here to make something sound cool. We are here to transform an idea and ideals into something people can believe in. To quote the great Bill Bernbach, "You can say the right thing about a product, and nobody will listen. You've got to say it in such a way that people will feel it in their gut. Because if they don't feel it, nothing will happen."

To do that takes incredible skill. It takes talent. And it takes courage.

It also takes a client.

The client is your sherpa. They are guiding you toward a great accomplishment, but you are the one who must achieve it. They will point out all of the things that have worked in the past, and all of the ways that people have failed. They will tell you what they want, and what they don't want. This is a wealth of information, and you should pay careful attention to all of it. But you will need to guide them, too.

When speaking with clients in discovery sessions, they will usually be quick to tell you all about the tangible benefits of their product or service. Go ahead and let them do it, and take good notes. Ask questions. You will need this information to help you justify the bigger idea of their brand that you will create.

“

As copywriters, our job is to breathe life into a vision. We are here to transform an idea and ideals into something people can believe in.

You want to find out what they think makes their brand great, and where they fall short. Why do they feel like they are the best brand in their industry, and why do they sometimes feel inferior to the competition? What you really want to know is what makes their brand special. What makes their brand matter?

This is what you will need to articulate or even define for the brand. Why it matters.

But be warned. Your goal cannot be to simply mirror the client, or solely aim to please them. You must push them into new and likely uncomfortable territory. You should make them a little nervous. And you should be nervous, too. If you are not nervous before presenting your ideas to your client, you haven't gone far enough. You are not presenting an idea that will make a difference. You haven't done your job.

> **"**
>
> **If you are not nervous before presenting your ideas to your client, you haven't gone far enough.**

If the idea is strong enough, the client will replace anxiety with excitement. And this is the holy grail of the client-writer relationship. If they are truly excited—like they can't wait to get this brand out there in the world—they become the strongest advocates for what you have created. They will do everything in their power and their budgets to promote your work. And there is no greater feeling than seeing your work out in the world, making a difference. For that to happen, you need your guide. You need the client.

The best clients are often the toughest ones. (Not to be confused with mean clients.) Tough clients push you to the edge. They make you nervous. It's because they care about their brand. They care about bringing a vision to life. Embrace them. Build trust. Then challenge them. They are not the Devil, but you should play the role of Devil's Advocate. It's the only way to get to the truth.

This is by no means an exhaustive list, but here are some items that you'll want to cover in your discovery sessions with clients:

- Where does the brand/product excel?
- Where does the brand/product fall short with consumers, and as compared to competitors?
- What are the top tangible benefits of the brand's product/service?
- What are the top emotional benefits of the brand's product/service?
- If they wanted the brand to be known for one thing not related to its product or services, what would that be? (Trust, safety, creativity, honesty, innovation, etc.)
- What do they want people to feel when they come in contact with the brand?
- How should the brand sound? (Casual and conversational, sophisticated and intelligent, etc.)
- If five years from now the brand was on the cover of [pick an industry-appropriate magazine], what would the headline be?

The discovery sessions are crucial to building a meaningful verbal brand identity. You must be able to derive tangible, intangible, and emotional benefits.

Don't be afraid to ask stupid questions. Act as if you've never heard of the company or even the industry before. (However, I recommend that you prepare the client for this kind of approach so that they don't assume that you are not very bright.) Tell them you are approaching this like a journalist. That some questions might seem remedial and sometimes repetitive, but that is by design to make sure you get to know every important intricacy of the brand. This is the time to get as much information as you possibly can. It is not ideal to go back to the client weeks down the road because you didn't get the information you needed.

As with every client meeting, come prepared. Look into the industry. Try to gain a solid understanding of the problems and opportunities of the industry and get familiar with terms and terminology. You want to approach this like a journalist, but you don't want to be ignorant. Asking one intelligent question using their own industry parlance can go a long way toward establishing immediate credibility and confidence.

Observation: The Superpower of Every Great Copywriter

You might assume that being a strong writer is all about style, understanding sentence structure, proper grammar and punctuation, and wit. Those are very helpful traits of any good writer. But the copywriter's most important skill is observation.

To make a connection, you must understand what is driving the desire for the connection in the first place. And the only way to do that is to observe. Look, watch, and listen.

One of the most celebrated lines of copy in the history of copywriting comes from famed copywriter and advertising executive David Ogilvy, written for a Rolls-Royce ad.

At 60 miles an hour the loudest noise in this new Rolls-Royce comes from the electric clock.

It works so well because Ogilvy took the time to observe. He noticed two crucial truths:

1. **Of the vehicle:** It possessed a very unique trait compared to other vehicles. Not just its fine finishes, smooth ride, or striking, famous hood ornament. When traveling at speed, the vehicle was uncommonly quiet.

2. **Of its place in the consciousness of the target society:** He noticed that the highest marks of luxury are often the most subtle. True luxury is not shouted from the rooftops. It is whispered among those who know it best.

The clock—not the premium leather or the high-performing engine—signaled ultimate luxury. The clock is the whisper heard round the world, so to speak.

That is observation in its sharpest focus.

“

The copywriter's most important skill is observation.

To hone one's observation skills, it must be a daily practice. Most copywriters just naturally observe the details of their surroundings, but intentional observation is the key. Spend a solid fifteen minutes watching fish in a fish tank. You'll soon see patterns and behaviors that repeat themselves. You will soon understand the differences and similarities between species.

I know that most manhole covers in Chicago come from Neenah, Wisconsin. This is because I purposefully looked at them on my daily commute and wanderings throughout the city. It might be inconsequential, but who knows, it might come in handy one day.

I make fast friends with dogs. This is because I watch their body language before and when I approach them. I listen to the sounds they make and feel their body weight shift when I scratch them in certain places. (Under the collar is usually a winner.) Babies and I like to look at each other. I've found that smiling with my eyes and raising my eyebrows forms a quick bond.

Daily observation is a subconscious way to train your brain to quickly come to an understanding. A sharp sense of observation creates a shorter, more informed path of identifying people's subtle desires and needs. And that is what creates a true connection. Anyone can point out the obvious. (Rolls-Royce is a status symbol.) The craftsman understands and points out the compelling, often emotional benefit. (The Rolls-Royce offers the ultimate luxury of quiet amid chaos.)

Observe daily. Pay attention to the details. Question their purpose.

Understanding the Essence of the Verbal Identity

The simplest way to understand the power of a verbal brand identity is to not read anything at all about a brand. Instead, think of a brand. Any brand. Then think about how it makes you feel.

- **Coca-Cola** makes me feel happy.
- **Pampers** makes me feel love.
- **Apple** makes me feel creative and modern.
- **Harley Davidson** makes me feel gritty, a little dangerous, and free.

I guarantee that if you were to take a peek into these brands' verbal identities, you would find those exact words or very similar words in each one of them.

That's not a coincidence. It's a carefully designed projection of how those brands want to appear and how they want you to feel when you interact with them.

Now consider a few brands that are large and profitable, but that you would be hard pressed to find anyone who has strong opinions about.

- **GE:** I know they make appliances and airplane engines, but I have no idea what they stand for or how they want me to feel.

- **Pepsi:** The last thing I can remember about Pepsi's verbal identity is "The choice of a new generation." That was a few generations ago. I would not consider Pepsi the chosen one of any generation, and nothing else comes to mind.

- **Mastercard:** No clue.

I would make a sizable bet that these brands have very weak, very outdated verbal identities. I would make another bet that the teams in charge of these brands all have different ideas and opinions about what their brand represents.

The verbal brand identity is designed for two audiences: the internal and the public. They hold equal weight, and they are influenced by and dependent on each other.

INTERNAL

From the startup to the Fortune 500 company, having internal alignment on the brand's verbal identity is vital. Without it, it's like telling someone a story with several different endings. Great for a *Choose Your*

Own Adventure book, but terrible for making a lasting connection with your target audience.

Over the lifespan of a brand, any number of people will be responsible for communicating the brand identity—from onboarding new employees and agency partners, to handling social media accounts, to advertising campaigns and talking to the press.

> **"**
> **The verbal brand identity is designed for two audiences: the internal and the public. They hold equal weight, and they are influenced by and dependent on each other.**

Everyone in the company should know exactly what the brand stands for, at all times. Ideally, in a word or two. Everyone should be able to rattle off the top three or four value propositions the brand or product offers. Everyone should be able to clearly articulate what makes their brand different from their top competitors. And everyone in the company should innately talk about the brand using a tone that is reflective of the brand's personality. If I'm shopping for a Rolls-Royce, I should be hearing some pretty sophisticated words. If I'm looking at a Harley, I should hear the word "badass" at some point in the sales pitch, at any location.

A verbal identity should be simple to understand and recite. It should fit on one page. It should be revisited annually and signed off on by the key stakeholders in the company. And whenever it gets updated in any way, it should be immediately circulated to everyone and discussed at length to ensure absolute clarity and alignment.

EXTERNAL

Consumers will never read your verbal identity deck. They won't read your brand narrative word for word. At best, they will know your name and your tagline, and maybe recall an ad campaign every now and then. But they will always know and remember how you make them feel.

Furthermore, in today's content-driven world, they will be exposed to your verbal identity all over the place. In social media posts, emails, videos, blog posts... it's never been more important to have a compelling and memorable voice and narrative. The reason is simple. People change. They change their behaviors and their habits. They change when they have children, buy a home, move, become empty nesters... What is important to them changes. But what is at the core of what they believe rarely changes. Your brand wants to establish what you believe quickly and firmly so that your customers can identify with your beliefs, quickly and firmly.

Communicating your brand's beliefs is all about writing a consistent and extensible verbal brand identity. Consistency so that you are there how they expect you to be there as they have always known you. Extensibility so that as they change, you are there to accompany them on their journey, and to help them take the next step, and the one after that.

Consistency

Think about some of your favorite brands. Chances are good that you get the same feeling from them whether it's a television ad, social media post, or billboard.

Skittles comes to mind. Every narrative they put out there, in all mediums, is consistently bright and colorful, light-hearted, and quirky. In a social media post for Halloween in 2024, Skittles showed their customers how to mix Skittles and M&Ms into the same bowl, creating a trick of a treat for unsuspecting candy grabbers. (Adding a layer of authenticity, the perpetrator tasted it, and was unafraid to show his disgust.) It's a perfect example of a brand identity—quirky, even a little unhinged—playing out across a medium perfectly suited to the narrative. Skittles' tagline, "Taste the Rainbow" supports it all because the brand is about so much more than the actual taste of the candy.

Once a brand's verbal identity is established, it is vital that it permeates every brand touchpoint consistently. It's the difference between a brand being dismissed and becoming unforgettable. Every marketer knows that repetition is a big factor in the success of any campaign, and there is no bigger campaign than the brand's overarching message. Consistency is key.

Extensibility

As noted in the Skittles example, the ability to extend the brand's identity is a big factor for modern brands, when the brand's message is being broadcast across so many different mediums. But here's the thing: The verbal identity goes far beyond just the message. The entire brand, including its products and services, is driven by its identity.

> **A strong verbal identity sets up a brand for future growth as a business.**

Apple started as a computer company before going on to become one of the most recognized and valuable brands in the world. They started from a place of incredible strength by formulating a powerful and extensible brand identity. Beginning with "Think Different" and codified over decades now, Apple's brand identity is how they were able to evolve from computers to software, photography, filmmaking, music, games, augmented reality... Their brand identity is why we believe they can do all of these things at the highest level. Because they stay true to the core position that they established and continue to hold—Creative and Modern. Beginning with "Think Different," all of their content and all of their storytelling is creative and modern.

This is why so much thought and care should go into a verbal brand identity. It's not just a marketing tool. A strong verbal identity sets up a brand for future growth as a business.

A modern brand's verbal identity must fulfill the following conditions:

- **Have a crystal-clear point of view that can be expressed in one or two words:** Coca-Cola = Happy; Apple = Creative, Modern; Disney = Magic
- **Achieve alignment with internal teams:** it can be easily recalled and recited verbatim, with the correct information and proper tone
- **Be consistent:** no matter where consumers come in contact with the brand, it leaves them feeling the same way
- **Be extensible:** while remaining consistent, modern brands must have the ability to dive into new stories and categories that are aligned with the overall brand position

Now, let's get into it.

STEP 1

Positioning

Positioning comes first.

Even if you don't have a name for your brand or product yet, start with positioning.

Before you go down the rabbit hole of competitive analysis, start with positioning.

There is a very good reason for this, and it is because consumers buy on beliefs. Even more so with up-and-coming generations (your future buyers). If you haven't watched Simon Sinek's TEDx talk, "Start With Why," where he speaks at length about Apple's positioning, you must. It is a simple and powerful formula that helps us understand how a brand's beliefs are the single most impactful way that consumers identify with a brand, regardless of what they sell.

When you define the brand's position, it can influence the name of the brand itself. It might lead to a new name, reinforce an existing name, or call into question whether or not the name is appropriate for the brand's core position. The same goes for the competition. A well-defined position can eliminate competition, or raise the possibility of new competitors that were never considered before.

Go big. This is the time to imagine what your brand will stand for regardless of what you intend to sell.

When Walt Disney planned Disneyland, he went big. The original site for the park was 160 acres. Other theme parks at the time (although they weren't called that—that was Disney's creation) were typically between ten and twenty acres. He did this not because he wanted to create a really big amusement park. He did this because he wanted to create magic. Another world. Not just a very large collection of carnival rides. Walt Disney believed in magic—that was his position. It just so happens that to create that magic, he needed a lot of acreage.

> **"**
>
> **This is the time to imagine what your brand will stand for regardless of what you intend to sell.**

Think about your brand. If you wanted it to be described in one or two words, what would those words be? Gather the client and your team and grab a few stacks of sticky notes. Ask everyone to write a word (or two) that describes how you want your customer to feel, one per sticky note. Encourage the team to push the boundaries. After writing each one, the team member should say it out loud, peel off the sticky note and stick it on the table. (It's important to say it out loud–as this might spark ideas in others.)

After about 5–10 minutes people might get quiet, because they are running out of ideas. Write "Yes" and "No" on a whiteboard. Gather up all the sticky notes and, one by one, read them to the group. Ask those who wrote each word to give their reasoning as to why they want the customer to feel that way about the brand. Ask the group if each word is a "Yes" or a "No." Some might be quick decisions but encourage debate. (Let's remember observation here. Look for passion when people are talking about the words–both those who are defending their choices and those who violently object. Take notes. Passion points us toward beliefs.)

Place each note in the "Yes" or "No" columns according to the discussion. A few "Maybes" are OK, but keep them to a bare minimum. We're in the stage where we want to be decisive.

When you're done, ask each person to vote for three from the "Yes" category that they feel the most strongly about. Thank them for their time, take a photo of the whiteboard, and retreat to your den.

Take ten to twenty minutes to write down what you heard and felt. Not necessarily about the individual words but your overall takeaways from the discussion. Because you're a writer, and because you have the superpower of observation, these thoughts could prove vital toward your work in articulating the brand position, both internally and externally.

Next, take all of the "Yes" and "Maybe" words and write them down in descending order according to how many votes each one received. You should have a good list of five to ten "Yes" options and two to three "Maybes." These are the strongest indicators of what your client believes their brand position to be. From here, you'll derive two to three candidates for the final brand position. But don't be afraid to include one or two of your own. Be sure to keep the photograph of the sorted whiteboard handy—you can use much of it to help with the rest of the verbal brand identity, including the Brand Promise, Brand Values, and Tone of Voice.

If I think about Nike, I think about a brand that makes me feel like I am an athlete. Some of those words might be these:

Empowered
Fast
Victorious
Agile
Healthy
Strong

These are all good ways to describe how someone might feel when they feel like an athlete. With a little lateral thinking, we can take those words to come up with another word that encompasses what we believe Nike is providing on a holistic level.

Nike's one-word brand position is: **Performance**.

Performance is what makes an athlete, an athlete. Performance is what Nike products offer to help you be the best athlete you can be.

Consumers are not necessarily asking for Performance. They are looking for attractive, high-quality shoes, pants, and hoodies. But if Nike focused solely on what the consumer wants, they would not have come to Performance. Instead, they might have come up with Gear or Equipment or Activewear. Yet, it is Performance that endears the brand to the consumer. And that's what we are looking for in a brand position.

Airbnb is another good example. To have the best travel experience possible, I want to feel like I am getting an authentic cultural experience. Nobody wants to feel like they are stuck in a tourist trap. Some words to describe those feelings might be the following:

Local

Comfortable

Safe

Relaxed

Happy

Adventurous

These are all ways to describe how someone wants to feel when they are somewhere new and unfamiliar, but excited to explore. Just like Nike doesn't position itself as Activewear, Airbnb doesn't position itself as a place to rent a vacation house.

Airbnb's one-word brand position is: **Belonging**.

When we travel, we want to feel like we belong there, even if we know it's not true. We want to eat at the restaurant the locals go to. We want to visit the areas where people can relax and connect with each other over real conversation. We don't want to be ignored, brushed off, or taken advantage of. That is belonging. Airbnb fosters this sense of belonging with unique places for rent in local neighborhoods where they encourage the hosts to offer some insider information about where to go, what to eat, and where to avoid.

Zoom isn't a conference calling app. It is **Connectivity**.

LEGO isn't a toy. It is **Creativity**.

Google isn't a search engine. It is **Knowledge**.

Think about how you want your brand to make people feel. Not how about how your product or service fits into their lives, or how you want them to use your product, but the emotions you want to spark in them. Describe that feeling in one or two words until you have a list of about five to ten. Revisit the sticky notes and include those.

When you have your list, start making associations. Look at the entire list, and think of emotional, empowering, and tangible words that can encompass the majority of your list. It should be easy to understand—something that anyone could hear and immediately identify with. It should indicate immediate value.

If you have one, slam dunk word, go with it. If you're struggling with two to three potential words, go ahead and move forward. You can always come back to it once more of your brand begins to take shape. If you have four or more words, it's too many.

Your word (or two or three words) are your new brand position in its purest form. This is what you are offering. Something that will be useful in making someone's life better.

Everything else will flow from this.

STEP 2

Brand Promise

The one-word brand position is a mostly internal tool. Although it can manifest in actual brand language and even campaigns, it is really there as a North Star to guide the rest of the brand through its development and evolution. As we move forward, we'll edge closer toward consumer-facing brand language.

The Brand Promise is a brief statement of what your brand will deliver to anyone who decides to engage with it. It is based on the one-word position but with added context of what makes this particular brand unique and valuable. It can be direct and factual or ethereal and malleable. But it must be inspiring. It can be somewhat of a mission statement, but it should relate to the products or services of the brand, not just what we want to accomplish in the broader sense of the world.

Nike's brand promise is: **To bring inspiration and innovation to every athlete in the world.**

It is a beautifully crafted statement that answers the call both internally and externally.

To consumers, Nike promises inspiration to be the best athletes they can be, whether that's from Nike's products, motivational advertisements, or the many clinics and foundations Nike supports around the world. They also promise innovation, from the groundbreaking waffle runner shoe to new sustainable fabrics. Sometimes they do both in one product, such as the Nike Pro hijabs to both inspire and innovate for Muslim female athletes.

For internal audiences, Nike's brand promise ensures that every decision, from product development to marketing, is guided to be consistent with the purpose of the brand itself—Performance.

If you take the two core elements of the Nike brand promise, you'll see how it ladders up to their brand position: **Inspiration + Innovation → Performance**

One could debate whether Nike has always lived up to its brand promise. They've had good years and bad ones. But it has been and remains one of the top athletic companies in the world. And they have had such great success, in part, because of a powerful, clear, and timeless brand promise.

Powerful

Every brand promise should be written with conviction. Like the brand position, the brand promise can be a mostly internal tool. So the copywriter should not be afraid to use force. Write as if this brand really will change the world. Swing for the fences. As architect Daniel Burnham said, "Make no little plans. They have no magic to stir men's blood and probably will not themselves be realized."

Clear

The two most common mistakes copywriters make when writing a brand promise are these: (1) Using too many words, and (2) Trying to fit everything their brand aims to do or offer into one statement. These problems are related, and this is why we start with a brand position. Stay as close to your brand position as you can, while adding a layer of depth and personality. While we haven't yet explored Tone of Voice, this is the perfect time to start writing how you want your brand to sound.

> **"**
>
> **Every brand promise should be written with conviction.**

Timeless

The best brand promises are built to last beyond any campaign, tagline, or logo redesign. It is important to write a brand promise in a way that cuts right to the heart of the ethos of the brand. It should be independent of any trend, time period, or individual product or service. All of that will change. The brand promise should guide the company and its customers far into the future. Now, if a company decides to completely pivot and fundamentally rebuild, then the entire brand is going to change, too. Probably even the name.

Let's look at Nike's brand promise one more time.

"To bring inspiration and innovation to every athlete in the world."

It is powerful... "every athlete in the world"

It is clear... "To bring inspiration and innovation"

It is timeless... There will always be athletes, and they will always need inspiration and innovation, regardless of the product or service.

When it's time to unveil your brand promise to your client, Brand Director, CEO, CMO, whomever... do not be afraid. Deliver it like a preacher—clearly and with conviction. It is far better to offer a brand promise that needs to be scaled back rather than one that doesn't go far enough. Inspire them. Cement your role as a brand soothsayer now, and everything you deliver after that has a much better chance of succeeding. If you underwhelm right from the start, if you do not capture the heart and soul of the brand, it will be much harder to convince your audience that you are the person to articulate their brand into the future. You will be much more likely to be second-guessed; micro-managed; or worse, replaced.

No pressure.

"

When it's time to unveil your brand promise to your client, do not be afraid. Deliver it like a preacher—clearly and with conviction.

STEP 3

Brand Values

The modern consumer (particularly younger generations) make their buying decisions and form brand loyalties based on far more than the quality of the product or how much it costs. Today's consumers want to know that their time, energy, and money are supporting a better world. Every soulful brand must be explicit in how they view their impact and legacy.

These are the Brand Values.

Brand values most often appear to the consumer on the company website, in the About or Company pages, and they can add great value to those who are searching for them. However, values are more important as internal guidelines for those responsible for product development and communications. Consumers will most often feel the brand values more than they will see them. That doesn't mean they are unimportant to articulate. Everyone in the company will need to understand and align with the brand values for it to take a meaningful place in consumers' lives. We want to be able to draw correlations between the brand's values and how business decisions are made, which manifests in product and service offerings.

When working with the client to establish brand values, hold them accountable. If they claim that they care deeply about supporting local communities, but they outsource the lion's share of their operations, start asking questions (without being combative). Brand values must be truthful and iron-clad. The modern consumer will quickly abandon brands who don't walk the talk.

Make sure the right people are in the room. You want the top brass, including founders and CEOs, but you also want key cultural influencers, like those responsible for messaging, product innovation, and even hiring decisions. Ask your client to identify these people and others who drive the vision of the brand.

I use a simple formula when asking clients about their brand values: **What we value + Why we value it + How it manifests in our business**

“

The modern consumer will quickly abandon brands who don't walk the talk.

What We Value

Most clients will have an idea of the brand's values. Your job is to dig into them. Start by asking for a simple list of their company values. (If they don't have them, ask them why they do what they do. As they describe it, write down words that broadly encapsulate what they are saying. For example, if the client says, "We do this because consumers are being tricked into buying unhealthy food," you might write down Transparency, Integrity, and Healthy Living as options for their brand values.) Once you have a list, yours or theirs, ask the room to discuss them and note the three to five that seem the most important and most true to what they do.

Why We Value It

What makes each brand value valuable to the company? How does the brand value benefit the customer? How does it influence the vision of the company? How does this brand value set the stage for a successful future? How does it help create a better world for their employees and their children? It is often with these questions that we learn what is a desired value, and what is actually true.

How It Manifests In Our Business

How are the brand values specifically activated through our products and services? Does the brand participate in any philanthropic activities that actualize our brand values? How do our brand values help us make critical decisions about the business, like sourcing, product development, hiring, and internal policies?

Once you have your values and all of the supporting information, choose three to five of them using the following criteria:

- Does this value directly impact the brand's products or services?
- Do the majority of stakeholders in the future of the brand agree on this value being important to the future of the business?
- Does this value align with the brand position and brand promise?

The answer to each of these questions should be "yes." If it's not, either the value is not true or important, or your brand position and promise need adjusting.

Now write the brand values, using the same formula: **What we value + Why we value it + How it manifests in our business**

Don't try to be too pure, infallible, or immaculate. In fact, most of the time sticking to one's values will come at the expense of other ideals. Be honest about it. Be direct. For example, if the environment is important to your brand, but it means making certain sacrifices, you might write something like this:

> ***We value a healthy planet.*** *Like every business, we want to be successful. But not at the cost of future generations. That's why we source the most sustainable materials possible for our products from all over the world, even though we prefer to buy materials from local communities when they meet our standards.*

The message is clear. A healthy planet is one of our top priorities. It might come at a cost. But we support our local economies when it makes sense.

This is straightforward, honest, and beyond reproach. It contains valuable information for both internal and external audiences. With two to four more of these, we have core brand values that guide the company and its communications, and will ultimately permeate through to the consumer at every touchpoint.

STEP 4

Mission/Vision

The Brand Mission and Brand Vision are similar and related, but they serve two different purposes.

The Brand Vision is an aspirational statement derived from the Position and Brand Promise that guides the brand toward what it wants to achieve in the next five to twenty-five years.

The Brand Mission details what your company does today that will help it achieve the vision in the future.

We write mission and vision statements so that the brand has a clear roadmap, with a beginning point and an end state. These two items inform not just communications and marketing, but can help guide the entire brand strategy, down to product development and service offerings.

Some brands choose to be very forward with their mission and vision statements, publishing them prominently on their websites, in advertisements, or even directly on the products they sell. Others are more reserved, tucking them inside company about pages or in downloadable strategic plans or press packets.

Soulful brands tend to make them more visible. Either way, the brand must be accountable for the mission and vision for it to hold any weight or serve any purpose at all. Brands can do a lot of damage, both in consumer perception and internally among its people if the mission and vision are not followed religiously. For that reason, it is wise to revisit mission and vision statements every year.

> **“**
>
> **We write mission and vision statements so that the brand has a clear roadmap, with a beginning point and an end state.**

Let's start with the vision.

There are two simple guiding principles to writing a vision statement:

1. **Make it aspirational and future-oriented.** If we revisit the brand position and brand promise, we have a good head start. Now push further out. In the next five to twenty-five years, what would we hope to achieve if we are successful beyond our promise and our goals? How would we impact the most people possible? How would our brand change the world for the better?

2. **Make it ambitious, but achievable.** We're swinging for the fences here, but we want to make sure we don't set impossible goals. This is important for consumers to believe in us and

support us, as well as for our internal teams to stay motivated and focused.

We write the vision first because it helps us understand what we will need to do to get there, which is the mission statement.

The mission follows a simple three part formula:

1. **What** the company is offering today
2. **Who** we are doing it for
3. **Why** we are doing it

The National Geographic Society offers a good example of both mission and vision statements, and how they work together.

Their mission is: *The National Geographic Society uses the power of science, exploration, education, and storytelling to illuminate and protect the wonder of our world.*

Their vision is: *By 2030, the National Geographic Society will be known globally for its bold and impactful Explorer-led programs that spark curiosity in hundreds of millions of people, inspiring them to learn about, care for, and protect our world.*

You will notice in the mission that they are addressing:

- **What they offer today:** science, exploration, education, and storytelling
- **Who they are doing it for:** our world ("our" meaning all of us)
- **Why they are doing it:** to illuminate and protect

Following the mission is the vision, wherein they address:

- **Aspirational and future-oriented:** *spark curiosity in hundreds of millions of people, inspiring them to learn about, care for, and protect our world*
- **Ambitious but achievable:** *be known globally for its bold and impactful Explorer-led programs*

When viewed together, you get a great sense of what the brand offers today and why, and what they will achieve in the future when the mission is fulfilled.

The mission and vision statements are most commonly dictated by the client, and are likely something they have already put some time and effort into. However, it is important to have everyone aligned. When you are meeting with your client during discovery sessions, be sure to ask about these items and pressure test them. Ask leading questions, like a journalist, to make sure that the "whys" and "hows" are clear, true, and achievable. Even if the client already has these written down, the chances are good that you can help refine them, either in what they say or how they are saying it.

STEP 5

Brand Persona & Tone of Voice

With our Positioning, Brand Promise, Brand Values and Mission/Vision in place, it's time to shape the brand's personality. Start with the Brand Persona.

Think of your brand as a person. If you met this person at a cocktail party, how would you describe them? Are they smart? Funny? Are they kind? Are they somewhat distant, or attentive and engaging?

> **"The persona is the expression of the brand's soul.**

The brand persona is going to influence everything from the brand name and brand narrative (which ultimately develops into assets like website copy and advertising) to the brand's visual identity like logos and color palettes. The persona is vital to forming a long-term bond with the consumer. It is the expression of the brand's soul.

Think of some of the most recognizable and valuable brands in the world, and you'll quickly associate them with their personas.

McDonald's is bright and happy.

Jeep is rugged and adventurous.

Louis Vuitton is stylish and sophisticated.

By this point, you might already have a decent idea of your brand's personality type. But it's well worth the time and effort to pressure test your instincts.

The concept of "brand archetypes" is often attributed to Carl Jung, who theorized that humans have a collective unconscious, containing universal patterns of behavior and symbolism—archetypes. Marketers, as we do, borrowed this concept and applied it to branding to create distinct brand personalities.

There are the twelve commonly accepted brand archetypes:

1. **The Hero**
2. **The Ruler**
3. **The Everyman**
4. **The Outlaw**
5. **The Explorer**
6. **The Jester**
7. **The Caregiver**
8. **The Innocent**

9. **The Lover**

10. **The Magician**

11. **The Creator**

12. **The Sage**

Each of these archetypes has a goal.

1. **The Hero:** to improve the world
2. **The Ruler:** to create order
3. **The Everyman:** to belong
4. **The Outlaw:** to liberate
5. **The Explorer:** to discover
6. **The Jester:** to bring joy
7. **The Caregiver:** to protect others
8. **The Innocent:** to be happy
9. **The Lover:** to create intimacy
10. **The Magician:** to inspire wonder
11. **The Creator:** to provide uncommon value
12. **The Sage:** to impart wisdom

You might find that your brand crosses over into two or more personas. This is common, and also a common pitfall. In my experience, very few clients feel confident that they fit squarely into one persona. Try your best to make a case for one. Defining the brand in one persona provides focus. The more focused your persona, the easier it is for all audiences, internal and external, to understand and connect with the brand. A combination of two can work, but it's a slippery slope. Any more than two and you'll have a brand identity crisis on your hands. That's a direct path to a forgettable brand and a disaster in the making.

It can be helpful to see some well-known brands and their associated archetypes:

1. **The Hero:** Nike
2. **The Ruler:** Microsoft
3. **The Everyman:** IKEA
4. **The Outlaw:** Harley Davidson
5. **The Explorer:** Jeep
6. **The Jester:** Old Spice
7. **The Caregiver:** The American Red Cross
8. **The Innocent:** Coca-Cola
9. **The Lover:** Godiva Chocolate
10. **The Magician:** Disney
11. **The Creator:** Apple
12. **The Sage:** Google

This is a good time to take a look back at your brand position, brand promise, and brand values. This should give you a pretty strong indication of what brand archetype fits your brand. It's important to remember that you are not trying to please people, whether internally or externally. Your goal is to be true to the brand. Also draw from all of your meetings with the client. Often, the brand's leadership is a pretty straight line to the brand's archetype.

Tone of Voice

I've heard "tone of voice," "voice and tone,", "brand voice"... they are all the same thing. This is how you want your brand to sound, and the manifestation of the brand archetype. If your brand were a person, would the conversation be formal or chatty? Does your brand sound like a surfer or a stockbroker?

Start with your brand archetype. Once you have one (or two) chosen, use that to start coming up with a list of descriptor words that line up with the archetype. So, if you chose "Caregiver" as your archetype, a few descriptor words might be these:

- **Warm**
- **Approachable**
- **Informative**

You should have some indicators of tones from your observational superpower and the earlier discovery sessions with your client. Distill those indicators into descriptor words. Make a list of all of your descriptor words, then get ready to start whittling it down. Some cuts will be easy, like those that overlap. But the devil is in the details. Witty is not the same as funny, for example. Some cuts will be more difficult, but it is important that you come up with a manageable list.

In the end, you're going to want between three and five tone of voice descriptors. I prefer three. More than five, and you risk complicating the brand voice to the point that it becomes inconsistent and hard to follow. The brand (and you) will eventually use the tone of voice as a guide when creating any content. The more descriptors you have, the more difficult it's going to be to follow the guide. As a writer, it can be hard to remember that most people are not natural writers. It might come naturally to you to write in a brand's voice without even referencing tone of voice documentation, but most people will need it to make sure the brand is personable, recognizable, and consistent. Make it easy on them.

Once you have your list, write a description of each term. Make it as straightforward as possible. Then write some copy. Use what you've learned about the benefits of the brand's product or services as your source material, then describe those benefits using the tone of voice guide. You will come back to refine this once you've fleshed out the Unique Selling Propositions (USPs) but we'll get to that later. For now, write one example of the correct way to use each tone descriptor, describing a brand benefit and one example of the incorrect way. For example, if one of your descriptors is "conversational," write one good example of a conversational tone and one example that is more stilted or dry. But be careful to not go too extreme. Tone is often about subtlety. You want your guide to show the user how to implement tone when it's not so obvious.

Here are twenty tone descriptor words that might help you get started:

- **Approachable**
- **Authentic**
- **Bold**
- **Conversational**
- **Confident**
- **Dependable**
- **Energetic**
- **Friendly**
- **Honest**
- **Informative**
- **Inspiring**
- **Lighthearted**
- **Playful**
- **Professional**
- **Quirky**
- **Refined**
- **Relatable**
- **Serious**
- **Sophisticated**
- **Warm**

There is one important caveat to creating a tone of voice. The goal is not to create a tone that is groundbreaking or completely original to the brand. There are very few brandws that need such a thing. The goal is to provide easy-to-understand guidelines for people who will be creating content for the brand. Keep it simple and straightforward. Tone will naturally come through as the brand evolves.

Writing the Brand Persona

The brand persona deliverable is a one-page document that describes the brand's archetype and personality. Think of it like the opening page of a FBI case file you might see on TV.

I like to start with a photograph. I find a character that matches well with the archetype and tone of voice, and everything else that I've come to understand about the brand's personality through the work to date and the discovery sessions. TV and movie characters, even cartoon characters, work well because they are written as personas themselves. Pay attention to ethnicities and gender, as they can tend to create bias when viewed by the client.

For example, I did some brand identity work for a client whose purpose was to help other companies succeed. They weren't the Hero—instead, they helped their clients become the hero. This brand was the Sage with a touch of the Creator. They were highly intelligent and sophisticated but also quite affable. I chose the character "Q" from the James Bond series.

Next, write the narrative of that persona. There are plenty of ways to do this, but a few items you might want to cover include their goals and motivations, likes and dislikes, and their values. Include the brand archetype on the page, and the tone of voice descriptors. In the end it should be a relatively brief document that gives a full picture of the desired personality of the brand. This will be used by the client to ensure website content, advertising, social media content, and any other brand communications are consistent and on-brand across all platforms and subject matter.

STEP 6

Audiences

It might seem odd to just now be getting to audiences. It's true that audience research and definitions come earlier in many cases, such as product development. But for our purposes, I prefer to define the brand first. The reason for this is because a soulful brand must understand itself before figuring out how to connect with its audience. A soulful brand is birthed from a vision. It comes from passion, not the desire to please or to target. There will be plenty of time to target your audiences with future content and advertising campaigns, which will require plenty of audience profiling. Alas, we do have audiences, so we need to do a little work on them.

The job is to find out how the brand fits in our audiences' lives. A few words of warning here: Don't get too cozy with the audience. If you put too much stock in appealing to your audience, you risk producing milquetoast. You want your messaging to *align* with your audience, not mimic them. That being said, this is the time to step outside of your brand. Pretend your audiences have never heard of it.

> **You want your messaging to *align* with your audience, not mimic them.**

Let's keep this pretty simple.

Start with the people who dreamed up the brand in the first place. These are the visionaries, and they already know something about the brand's audiences. (That is due in no small part because the visionaries themselves are usually the prime audience for the brand in the first place.) Build a list of their target audiences, and add to that any audiences you think are good fits based on what you have come to understand about the brand and its products or services. You'll want to start by identifying the audience, then exploring the tangible benefits the brand provides to them. Keep your total number of audiences reasonable. Five is usually a good target, but fewer is fine, too. Keep the answers to these questions as straightforward as you can.

- **Who** would use these products (or services)?
- **What** problem(s) does our product solve for each of them?
- **How** would each of our audiences use our products?

- **How** are each of their lives better after engaging with our products?
- **Why** would each audience choose our products over the competitors?
- **What** might make each of our audiences look forward to our next product?

Now take your list of audiences and ask a different set of questions that pull at the emotional drivers—of the brand, not the product.

- **How** does seeing our brand or hearing its name make our audiences feel? (e.g., confident, happy, smart)
- **What** are some emotional benefits our brand provides to each audience? (e.g., removes stress, adds joy)
- **When** each audience thinks about our brand, what memories or associations do they have?
- **What** would our audiences miss most if our brand ceased to exist?

You should end up with a pretty good list of tangible and intangible benefits that your audiences will soon discover about your brand. Keep them handy.

There is another approach to align your brand with its audiences that can work well, particularly if you like working in a more formulaic way. Or, you can use it as a way to validate or whittle down your findings.

FOR: Describe your ideal target customer who is buying the product or service.

WHO NEED: Describe the customer's need or opportunity that will make a difference in their lives or business.

AND WANT: Describe the other factors, including and importantly emotional, that will influence their decision to buy from your brand (excluding price).

THE: Name of the product or company.

IS: Provide the category that the market associates with your product or service.

Eventually, this audience analysis is going to produce three important results.

1. **Help define our Unique Selling Propositions:** When we start to get into the details about our brand and products, we will want to dissect the benefits (value propositions) and organize them as to how they align with our audiences' needs and wants.

2. **Inform headlines, advertisements, and taglines:** Headlines, ads, and taglines all share a common requirement to be successful. They must address an audience's need—emotional or tangible—quickly and with very few words. By knowing about our audiences' needs, we can be sure to speak to them directly.

3. **Provide targeting criteria:** This doesn't necessarily help you with building the brand identity, but it will help your client in the future when it comes to marketing campaigns and lead

generation. They will end up getting much more granular with targeting, but it's an important benchmark to make sure marketing stays true to the brand identity.

The final product should look something like this:

Audience 1 (e.g., "Millennial Women")

- Most tangible benefit
- Second tangible benefit
- Third tangible benefit
- Most emotional benefit
- Second emotional benefit
- Third emotional benefit
- Best outcome of using our brand
- Second outcome of using our brand

At this point I'd recommend validating your findings. Your client is the obvious first step. They should be 100 percent aligned with what you've discovered, but encourage them to go beyond just the key decision makers. Product development teams, sales teams, and marketing teams are all good sources of validation as they are often closer to the heartbeat of the customer than many C-suite decision makers. You might also encourage them to validate your audience findings with select existing customers, if there are any, and other people they have trusted along the way to help shape the current brand.

STEP 7 Naming

Naming a brand is easily the most exciting part of building a brand. It's also the most difficult. It is equal parts business logic and emotional gymnastics. It's easy to fall in love with a name to the point you can't see anything else, only to find out that it's already trademarked or the client just simply doesn't "love" it. It's a rollercoaster ride through a fun house—thrilling, scary, and often bringing one to the brink of madness. I love it.

It probably seems really strange to consider naming the business this far down the path to a verbal identity. In my experience, the process of positioning the brand, fleshing out its values, writing a persona, and exploring audiences all leads to a more informed process of finding a name. With all of this intimate knowledge of the soul of the brand, naming will be an organic process, leading to a much more natural name for the brand.

If the brand doesn't yet have a name, this is the time to do it. Up to this point, use a placeholder name—something very generic. If the brand already has a name, this is when you want to ask your client if, after exploring and defining the soul of the brand, they still believe it's the right name. If you're working on a brand that is already well established in its industry, you're probably stuck with it. But it never hurts to ask.

> **"**
>
> **You shouldn't have to "sell" a great name. If it takes more than ten seconds to convince the client that it's a good candidate, it's probably too far of a reach, both for them and for the consumer.**

There are a few things to be aware of about naming:

1. **It takes time.** Sure, lightning may strike, but that's not common. Instead, it's going to be a process that will require dozens of hours of brainstorming and time to step away and rest. It's likely that it will take two or more rounds to finalize a name. Clients are going to be very critical about the potential name of their vision—as they should be.

2. **95 percent of your name ideas are going to be trash.** Naming is often a numbers game. You are going to want dozens of viable options to start. Most names that you like will be disqualified quickly by a simple trademark search. (Never present a name without at least

Googling it paired with the brand's industry.) Many names you like on Thursday, you'll hate on Monday. Like I said, madness.

3. **You shouldn't have to "sell" a great name.** It should be obvious that the name(s) you recommend are a great fit for the brand. If it takes more than ten seconds to convince the client that it's a good candidate, it's probably too far of a reach, both for them and for the consumer. That being said, it doesn't have to make perfect logical sense. It just has to fit.

Let's look at some brand names that have both soul and meaning.

Google

Derived from "googol," the term for ten to the power of hundred, it symbolizes the company's mission to handle and organize immense amounts of information. The name cuts to the core of what they do.

It's also a little goofy. In the early days, at least, Google was something of a band of misfits in an industry of unrestricted opportunity. The name perfectly encapsulates their early culture and values.

It's definitive. This is the holy grail of naming. "Googling" something means that you are going to use this specific brand to accomplish a common and necessary task. For those of us old enough to remember, a few other brand names that achieved this rarefied air include Xerox, Band-Aid, Q-Tip, and Sharpie. Having a great product doesn't hurt, but the name transcends the utility.

Duolingo

Like Google, the name is deeply rooted in its purpose. And it accomplishes this in two ways. First, the app is intended to help you become bilingual, or to learn two languages at once. Secondly, it's a collaborative and interactive approach that provides guidance and feedback. It takes two to tango, as they say. Or in this case, to lingo.

Duolingo celebrates language and its name does the same thing. It's lyrical, fun, and joyful, and just a little bit complicated—precisely reflective of the industry and their entire brand presence and tone. When you see the whole package in their branding, messaging, and marketing, it's perfect.

Impossible Foods

How did they do that? When Impossible Foods first came to market, most people's reactions were along the lines of, "This tastes like a real burger!" The customer experienced awe and wonder seeing the impossible become possible. The folks at Impossible Foods knew this could happen, and they wanted it to happen, so they chose a name that would set the expectation before the first bite. It was a brilliant strategic move.

It has also redefined a category. Before Impossible Foods, most restaurants would list "veggie burger" or "black bean burger" on the menu. After Impossible Foods, menus started listing "Impossible burger" instead. The product is innovative, and the name cements its status as such.

All of these names are successful because they are full of meaning. They all achieve the following:

- Speak directly to the core of the brand's mission and values (Purpose)
- Quickly define the product or service (Value)
- Reflect the company's persona (Personality)

One of my favorite naming projects came about in 2019, when I was approached by a Chicago news reporter who was starting a summer camp for disadvantaged kids. During her time reporting on the city, she had visited and spoken with hundreds of such kids. She learned that many of them hardly ever left their neighborhood and, consequently, they couldn't see beyond their conditions. They didn't have an expansive view of their world. Many of them had never seen Lake Michigan before, even though it was just a few miles away. In her mind, if you couldn't see, you couldn't imagine anything beyond what was right in front of you. She wanted to change that.

She teamed up with a local camp situated on a lake to host week-long camp experiences for disadvantaged Chicago children. There would be fishing and canoeing, hiking and confidence building activities... everything wonderful about a camp those who have been fortunate enough to experience it might expect. In her mind, if the kids could expand their view, even for just a little bit of time, they would be able to dream bigger. She needed a name.

Over the course of several conversations and discovery sessions, I learned enough to put together criteria for an approach, highly abbreviated below.

- The name should indicate the impact this camp can have on the kids
- It should be localized to the Chicago/Midwest region
- The camp would be on a lake, and the name should be reflective of the kids' nearest natural wonder, Lake Michigan

There is a weather phenomenon well-known by everyone who lives in Chicago (and elsewhere around the Midwest) called the lake effect. It's most commonly felt in winter, when Lake Michigan creates localized snowstorms. You might get several inches of snow near the lake and virtually no snow once you leave its climate region. It creates a localized impact–just like my client was hoping to do for these kids.

We named the camp **Lake Affect**.

With a deep understanding of the goals of the brand and the name itself, we were able to satisfy our criteria:

- The name should indicate the impact this camp can have on the kids

  By changing "effect" to "affect," we made sure it was known that this place would have a life-long impact on the kids. Perhaps even change their lives.

- It should be localized to the Chicago/Midwest region

The term "lake effect" was widely known in the region, carrying cultural significance to the Chicago/Midwest area.

- The camp would be on a lake, and the name should be reflective of the kids' nearest natural wonder, Lake Michigan

  Using the word "Lake" was an obvious nod to the camp being on a lake, and the full name Lake Affect was directly related to Lake Michigan.

To support the idea that even a small change could make a big difference, we attached the tagline, "Ripples make waves."

I do not know if the camp is still active. But I do know that when it launched, it indeed made waves—the good kind.

The key to a good name is to truly understand the purpose and value of the brand itself. I would have never come up with "Lake Affect" without digging deep to find the story behind the brand, and without asking many questions about why the brand mattered so much to my client.

When it comes to brainstorming name options, there are too many approaches to count. I'm sure there are some very good books already written that are only about naming. So instead of offering a step-by-step, I'll just leave you with a few pointers.

- Make "buckets" to fill up with names. Somewhere between three and five buckets based on the brand position, brand promise, values, and persona.

- Think sideways. When you have your brand position established, think of terms and descriptors that relate to the position, not necessarily define the position. (For example, if the brand's position is Collaboration, something like "Chorus" might be a good candidate.)
- Thesauruses and AI chatbots can be really helpful, but they are better used as thought starters than where to find the actual name.
- You can explore common naming wellsprings, like words in foreign languages, Latin words, animals, and adjectives, but know that names that come from this method are usually either too on the nose or the opposite, i.e., requiring too much of an explanation.
- Get weird. Think of names that are totally out of left field. Chances are good you won't pick one of these as a name candidate, but it will lead you down some interesting and, at times, fruitful paths.
- On a similar note, think of names that would be terrible for the brand. Again, you probably won't choose one of these, but it can sharpen your focus while widening your horizons.
- Simple and straightforward is usually a winning combination. However, they are also some of the more difficult names to get legal clearance for, as most of them will be taken by other businesses in the client's industry.

When it comes time to pitch your names to the client, take great care in building the presentation. Since you are a copywriter, I don't need to tell you to triple check spelling, etc. But have a designer design it. You want to instill confidence in the client, and a bad design will do subconscious damage to your ideas.

I like to choose an image to go along with the name. Not for design purposes, meaning that the image isn't to suggest a brand design direction, but rather to help set the tone for the name. Each name should be preceded by the category (or bucket) for the name; a very brief description of why the category is appropriate; and three to four bullet points that will support the name idea. Next, present the name by itself first (along with the image, if you choose). It should then be quickly followed by a very brief description of why the name is appropriate for the brand, and three bullet points that highlight why the name works.

I have found that ten to twelve names for the first round is about right, and five to seven additional or derivative names for the second round. Any more than that, and the client can get fatigued or confused, and it can suggest that your names lack conviction. Put a strong candidate first. Follow with a few names that might be "maybes." Put your "hot list" in the middle. You want to start off with a bang, then build momentum. Most clients want a few ideas to kill so that they feel like they are part of this important process. Those usually happen in the front or back of the list.

Remember that, like the entire verbal brand identity itself, we want to communicate Purpose, Value, and Personality.

One final note: The best names are versatile. Meaning that they are not boxed in with a name so specific that it will require modifications or a sweeping change as the brand grows and the products diversify. For example, when Waste Management moved beyond trash collection into recycling and alternate fuel production, they had to change their name to "WM" which is odd, nondescriptive, and uninspiring.

STEP 8

Brand Narrative

It's time to write the Brand Narrative.

The brand narrative is the larger, in-depth story of the brand. Think of it like the About page on a company website. (In fact, the narrative can often be lifted and placed directly on the website About page.)

To help you get started, you can use the same formula outlined in the Audiences section:

FOR: Describe your ideal target customer who is buying the product or service.

WHO NEED: Describe the customer's need or opportunity that will make a difference in their lives or business.

AND WANT: Describe the other factors, including and importantly emotional, that will influence their decision to buy from your brand (excluding price).

THE: Name of the product or company.

IS: Provide the category that the market associates with your product or service.

This can help you focus on what you will want to cover, but it is not a narrative. The brand narrative should be written like the plot of a story. Plots have five components:

Exposition

The exposition introduces the setting, characters, background, timeline, etc. For brands, the exposition can include the brand's origin story, purpose, and values. Like any good story, it should capture the reader's attention quickly. So, look to focus on the catalyst of the brand's exposition, not necessarily the blow-by-blow of the brand's founding.

Rising Action

In a typical story, the rising action builds tension. For brands, the rising action can be identifying the problems the brand is looking to solve, or the opportunities the brand opens up for its customers.

Climax

The climax is the story's turning point, usually the moment of highest tension or excitement. The climax for a brand narrative is where/how the brand delivers on its promise, solves the problem, and achieves a breakthrough.

Falling Action

The falling action is the part of the story that resolves the tension and starts moving toward closure. For brands, this is about showing a state of change. What is different now that the customer has chosen the brand? This part of the narrative is vital to strengthening relationships and establishing credibility.

Resolution

The resolution wraps up the story and provides closure while pointing to what comes next. In the brand narrative, this is where we can establish our brand's vision for the future, while demonstrating the ongoing/lifetime value of choosing the brand.

> **"**
>
> **The brand narrative should be written like the plot of a story.**

Before you get started with your brand narrative, keep a few things in mind.

1. **The narrative should be written in the brand tone.** This is not material for an investor pitch. This is a place to let the brand voice sing. That being said, be selective about where and how often you infuse it.

2. **Resist the urge to be overly self-promotional.** Yes, this is all about the brand, but it should be written genuinely to help the reader understand the brand, not urge them to rush out and buy the brand.

3. **Brief is usually better.** In some cases an exhaustive history of the brand might be appropriate, particularly if it is a legacy brand and if its history is important to understanding its future.

> But these days, people don't read a ton. Modern brands tend to keep brand narratives tight.

Warby Parker is, undoubtedly, a soulful brand. And you don't have to look any further than their brand narrative for proof. Here it is, from the History page of their website:

> *Every idea starts with a problem. Ours was simple: Glasses are too expensive.*
>
> *Our founders were students when one of them lost his glasses on a backpacking trip. The cost of replacing them was so high that he spent the first semester of grad school without them, squinting and complaining. (We don't recommend this.)*
>
> *The others had similar experiences and were amazed at how hard it was to find a pair of great frames that didn't leave their wallets bare. Where were the options?*
>
> *It turns out there's a simple explanation. The eyewear industry is dominated by a single company that has been able to keep prices artificially high while reaping huge profits from consumers who have no other options.*
>
> *Warby Parker was started to create an alternative. By circumventing traditional channels, designing glasses in-house, and engaging with customers directly, we're able to provide higher-quality, better-looking prescription eyewear at a fraction of the going price.*
>
> *We believe that buying glasses should be easy and fun. It should leave you happy and good-looking, with money in your pocket.*

> *We also believe that everyone has the right to see. Approximately one billion people around the world need glasses but don't have access to them—so to help address this problem, we work with a handful of partners worldwide to ensure that for every pair of glasses sold, a pair is distributed to someone in need. To date, over 15 million pairs of glasses have been distributed through our Buy a Pair, Give a Pair program.*
>
> *There's nothing complicated about it. Good eyewear, good outcome.*

If we look back at the elements of a plot, we can find them all in here.

Exposition: Including the initial problem statement (glasses are too expensive), the story about lost glasses and squinting through the first semester of grad school, and similar folks with the same problem of expensive eyeglasses.

Rising Action: The central tension is established with the evil dominant company artificially inflating prices at the expense of the consumer—our hero and his friends in the exposition.

Climax: Where the battle happens, by circumventing traditional channels, designing glasses in-house and engaging with customers directly.

Falling Action: In that Warby Parker is now providing higher quality, better-looking glasses at a fraction of the price.

Resolution: The new world is now a place where buying glasses is easy and fun and leaves you happy and with more money in your pocket. We also see a resolution for the future, through their *Buy a Pair, Give a Pair* program.

You will also notice that Warby Parker does an excellent job infusing their friendly, straight-shooter tone throughout the narrative, with pieces like *We don't recommend this* culminating in the last line: There's nothing complicated about it. *Good eyewear, good outcome.*

If you look around, you will find brand narratives of many kinds, from massive treatises to those of only a few sentences. It depends on the brand. Some might lean more on their history as a legacy brand, or newer brands might want more of a quick one-two punch. In any case the brand narrative, whether it appears word-for-word on a website or serves more of an internal guiding force, should ultimately encapsulate the purpose, value, and personality of the brand all in one shot. It is a crucial foundational asset and something of a measuring stick that should be called upon whenever the brand is launching a new product, developing a content or advertising campaign, and anything else that requires communicating the breadth of the brand.

STEP 9

Competitive Analysis

I will be direct. When it comes to developing a brand's verbal identity, I don't put a ton of stock in researching the competition. That is why it's ninth on my list of things to do, and why this section will be the shortest of the bunch.

The reason for this is similar to audience research in that over-analysis here can result in a diluted, forgettable, and soulless brand. I have seen far too many good ideas get whittled away when they start being measured against another brand.

I recommend competitive analysis for three reasons:

First, to make sure that you haven't accidentally pulled an idea from another brand. It happens to all of us—we absorb things throughout every day that seep into our subconscious. Every now and then, we unknowingly pull an idea from it and put it somewhere it doesn't belong. If it happens to you, don't panic. It is still likely a good idea. Either adjust it to better align with your brand, or use it as a springboard for something new and better.

Second, to make sure you're going to be better than the competition. Just about every brand has a competitor with a similar offering. Once I have my fundamentals in place, I like to see how other brands are attempting any similar messaging. How strongly or convincingly are they saying it? Oftentimes, competitive pressure makes our ideas a little bit better.

“

I have seen too many good ideas whittled away when measured against another brand.

Third, to prepare for the client presentation. In most cases, the client has a very deep understanding of their competition. Whether you are going to present the brand all at once or in parts, you want to know just as much as they do beforehand. If at any point the client raises questions or concerns about how you are positioning the brand relative to the competition, you must be prepared to answer quickly and with conviction and clarity.

It's never a bad idea to get a sense of how your brand identity is going to hold up next to the ones you're trying to outdo. You'll want to do this again when you are finished with the rest of the verbal identity. But take it with a grain of salt.

That's about all I have to say on competitive analysis.

STEP 10

Unique Selling Propositions

Eventually, we have to tell people what this business actually does, right? Now is the point where we start attaching the nuts and bolts of the brand's products and services. The Unique Selling Propositions (USPs, also often called Unique Value Propositions) are the specifics of the products or services that the brand offers, and how those products or services benefit the customer. It is a blend of art and science.

The USPs will ultimately be used to create content for the brand, such as website content, pitch decks, sell sheets, email campaigns, and anything else that needs a thorough, branded description of what they do.

You should have a full list of the brand's offerings and what makes each of those offerings unique and useful to its customers from your discovery sessions. If not, find a tactful way to ask for another meeting without making it look like you forgot to ask the first time.

The first thing I do is list out all of the significant offerings on a page, trying to keep them as straightforward and brief as possible.

For example, if the client told me that they offer "white glove service that goes far beyond anything that the competitors are doing for their customers," I write down *Industry-best service*. Or if they say that their app uses "large language models and AI to gather up-to-the-second data to help business leaders make important decisions," I write down *Superior data relevancy*. I'm boiling down the essential value that each offering provides to the customer.

Once I have the offerings listed out, I start to bullet the supporting information. So, underneath *Superior data relevancy*, I might write *large language models + AI* and, underneath that, *proprietary data sources* and so on. Keep in mind that the USPs are not all tangible. A soulful brand has emotional and cultural USPs as well. You will find these throughout your work so far, including the audience portion. List them out as well, also with supporting bullets.

Once you have all of the USPs listed with their supporting points, look for opportunities to consolidate. Ideally, you want no more than 5 USPs, if at all possible. Fewer means less that the brand needs to communicate, and less that the consumer needs to recall. As we know, the best brand identities are easy to communicate and easy to remember. Over time, the brand will hammer these points home through marketing and advertising so that they, along with the higher-level brand promise and values, are inextricably linked to the brand itself.

If you look at some of the most successful, soulful brands in the world, you'll experience easy recall that's been ingrained into your psyche for as long as you can remember.

Coca-Cola's USPs, for example, are a combination of taste, emotion, and culture. The drink is familiar and satisfying; it makes you happy; and it brings people together across generations and the world. Pretty simple, and very powerful.

> **Many brands offer very similar products or services, but how they communicate them makes all the difference.**

After consolidating as much as you can, you will need to go back to each USP to polish them up. Whereas it's easier to get them all on a page with straightforward language, each one of them needs to be written with the brand's persona and tone of voice. Many brands offer very similar products or services, but how they communicate them makes all the difference.

Coca-Cola and Pepsi are almost identical. They both offer a fizzy, caffeinated, similarly flavored drink, but their USPs are written very differently. Coca-Cola is classic, happy, and multi-generational. Pepsi is new, rebellious, and youthful.

Finally, revisit your audiences and note what message applies to which audience, in descending order of importance. So, if your first USP is most important to millennial working class males, then stay-at-home moms, then GenX empty nesters, list them under the USP in that order. There will be crossover—many messages will apply to the same audience, but they might differ in what message matters most to each of them.

So, your USPs should look something like this:

USP 1

- supporting point 1
- supporting point 2
- supporting point 3
  - audience 1
  - audience 2
  - audience 3

USP 2

- supporting point 1
- supporting point 2
- supporting point 3
  - audience 2
  - audience 3
  - audience 1

When you're done, organize the USPs on a page left to right, with the left being the highest priority and the right being the lower priorities, in terms of what's most important to achieve the client's messaging goals.

Writing USPs can be deceptively challenging. It's easy to think that the brand and its products and services are totally unique. In all likelihood, as noted with the Pepsi and Coca-Cola example, your brand will share USPs with another. Plus, the client is going to want to see that their offerings are unique, even if, fundamentally, they are not. Remember your superpower of observation. Remember that details matter. Meaningful and memorable brands are those that communicate the best, even when their offering is as ubiquitous as sugar water.

STEP 11

Headlines

Writing headlines is a fantastic way to distill USPs into customer-facing copy that begins to crystallize the brand's identity. Until this point, most of what we've written is a bit of navel-gazing—not just for us but for the client, too. Here, we can air it out.

Look around for industry publications that would be appropriate places for your brand to appear in an advertisement or article. I recommend a variety, from small, focused publications to the biggest ones. For example, a B2B client might be featured in trade publications that focus on specific, technical aspects of the industry, all the way up to widely circulated magazines that cover industry-leading trends, like *Forbes*. Newspapers, magazines, online publications, and blogs all work. Three to five should do. Write down the name of the publication and a one- to two-sentence description of what it covers and how, and at whom it's targeted.

Back in our discovery sessions, you might remember that we asked the client: *If five years from now the brand was on the cover of [pick an industry-appropriate magazine], what would the headline be?* Dust that off, and use it as your starting point. Then start writing headlines for each publication.

> **Headlines should align with the brand narrative.**

For the more niche publications, refer to your USPs. Write descriptive headlines about your USPs that address the publication's primary areas of focus. Use your brand persona and tone of voice to give them personality.

For the larger publications, use your positioning and brand promise to write more sweeping headlines about how your brand is uniquely solving industry problems or creating opportunities.

In both cases, the headlines should align with the brand narrative.

Don't stop until you have about twenty good headlines for each publication. Then pressure-test them.

I like to use the billboard test. Imagine driving 65 mph down the highway, when you look up to see a billboard. You only have about two to three seconds to read it, understand it, and consider what it's trying to tell you. There are four qualifications to pass the billboard test:

1. **Does it grab my attention?** Is there something in the headline that immediately catches my eye? It might be a fun turn of phrase, a unique play on words, or a thought-provoking statistic. Successful headlines pull you in, and fast.

2. **Do I understand it?** Is it written clearly, without a bunch of jargon? Simply put, does it make immediate sense, or do I have to rely on any prior knowledge I might have about the brand, product, or industry to get it?

3. **Is the USP clear?** If I am the target audience, do I quickly realize what the headline is offering me and why it would be valuable to me?

4. **Does it address the brand's Purpose, Value, or Personality?** Every headline doesn't have to communicate all three of our brand qualifiers, but each one must include at least one of them.

Get rid of any headlines that don't pass the billboard test. Refine the ones that are good but could be better.

There are some pretty standard ways to write a good headline. They are not totally necessary, and a great headline doesn't need to follow along, but here are some strategies that have proven to be helpful:

- Keep it brief
- Ask a question
- Use numbers, statistics, or specifics
- Tug on people's emotions

- Use surprise or contradiction
- Create FOMO and/or a sense of urgency
- Require the reader to make a "leap" (Walk them right up to the punchline, but don't give it to them. This can be a little risky because it's not always clear, but when done right, the reader will remember it because they solved the riddle.)

Remember the headline from the Rolls-Royce ad?

At 60 miles an hour the loudest noise in this new Rolls-Royce comes from the electric clock.

At 60 miles an hour grabs my attention. I want to know what happens. It addresses a USP. It communicates Purpose (luxury), Value (a quiet ride), and Personality (understated sophistication). It requires the reader to make a leap, but a very short one. And although a little on the long side, it's just brief enough to be a successful billboard.

Pick out the best three headlines that you've written for each publication. Show them to a cross-section of your peers and trusted advisors. Do not show them only to writers. We're all too impressed with our own abilities to be objective. Instead, choose designers, executives, marketing people, your husband or wife, your parents, your kids even. Get a sense of which headlines work the best, in their opinion. But you should ultimately make the final call, as you know the brand and the client best. Choose two headlines for each publication.

When presenting headlines to a client, I like to display a cover of the publication with the headlines next to it, big and bold. If you have the time and good designer on hand, you could impose the headline on the publication itself. However, sometimes it can be a little distracting, as the client might be influenced by other headlines on the page that might distort the context of yours. I usually present them in order from the niche to the mainstream publications. It's easier to warm them up with more straightforward, USP-based headlines before getting to the bigger, splashier ones.

The headlines deliverable is a big moment. It's usually the first time the client sees their verbal brand identity coming to life in context. It can be a little nerve-wracking, but it's a ton of fun. Especially when the client starts to get excited. You'll see it in their faces immediately. You shouldn't have to explain the headlines at all, but if the client asks questions about them, be ready to point to one reason it works so well, and that's it. Over-explaining your headlines makes them appear complicated and unsuccessful. If the headline doesn't work, ask why. You're building up to a tagline—one of the most important brand assets you can write.

STEP 12

Tagline

Do some Googling, and you'll find more debate than you can read in a lifetime about taglines. Are they necessary? (Absolutely.) What's the difference between a tagline and a slogan? (Not much.) After many years in this business, what I believe is that the tagline can be the single most impactful line of copy you ever write for a brand.

The tagline, what should be the most creative yet distilled interpretation of the brand, is a line of copy that can do more for a brand than any website, white paper, or advertising campaign could ever hope to do. It immediately sets the purpose, tone, and value proposition for the brand, all in one shot. It's an advertising campaign with an infinite lifespan. It should settle into the consciousness of your audience to the point that it becomes the brand's identity all in itself. An identity with a message. That's why the tagline should be written with great care and purpose. It needs to express the soul of the brand quickly, and it needs to last.

Let's look at some really successful taglines and what makes them work so well.

Betcha can't eat just one

With one of the most celebrated taglines in advertising history, Lay's tells you everything you need to know about their delicious, salty snack and their brand in just five words. What do we want in our snacks? We want to eat a lot of them, handful after handful. Lay's understands that. It's also an incredible job of telegraphing how craveable these chips are—almost planting the idea in consumers' minds by challenging them to deny themselves of a delightfully addictive snack. The unsung hero in this tagline, however, is Betcha. It strikes the perfect tone for a fun brand and aligns perfectly with its intended audience and their state of mind at the time of purchase.

> **The tagline needs to express the soul of the brand quickly, and it needs to last.**

Murder Your Thirst

Liquid Death exploded on the scene in the early 2020s with a masterclass in the branding of a commodity. What could be more ubiquitous than water? Yet, one look in the cooler at your local bodega, and it's clear there is something entirely different going on here. The sixteen-ounce aluminum cans (a first for water) and the aggressive graphics grab your attention. The tagline takes it to another level. We're not going to satiate your thirst. We're going to murder it, like you might murder a tall boy of your favorite beer after a long day. The purpose, tone, and value proposition are all there. And the tagline is expertly aligned with its young, outlaw-minded audience.

Eat Fresh

Subway introduced their tagline decades ago, and they still use it to this day, for good reason. Eat Fresh does two jobs really well. The first one is obvious, telling its audience the one thing they really need to know about the brand: The food is fresh. But there's something else in there: a hidden dig at the competition. By branding "fresh," Subway is also telling you that their competitors are not offering fresh food. Kind of like 7UP did with "the un-cola." Finally, the tagline, like Lay's, is a call to action, helping the audience align their own values with the brand.

I follow a few guidelines when I'm writing and evaluating taglines.

Include your brand's top value proposition or two. Even if it's subtle, the tagline should always connect to the primary reason the audience should consider or choose the brand.

Differentiate from the competition. As noted previously, I don't love focusing on the competition. But as a consumer-facing workhorse, it's not a bad idea to consider how your tagline will convince the consumer to buy your brand over the rest. ("The Un-cola," "Eat Fresh," for example.)

Take some poetic license. Throw grammar and proper sentence structure out the window. Write taglines lyrically so that it creates a brief moment of inspiration, and so that it sticks.

Keep it brief and simple. This should go without saying, but the faster you can get inside the consumer's head, the better. Very few lengthy taglines are successful. Those that are usually rely on making the consumer take a leap, like BASF's famous tagline: *At BASF, we don't make a lot of the products you buy. We make a lot of the products you buy better.*

Don't try to say everything all at once. I see many copywriters fail with taglines because they try to say too much. The tagline should hit the audience in the gut, not the brain.

One final note. If your client already has a tagline, consider the possibility of using it in a new way. A great example of this is Burger King. For decades, they used *Have it Your Way*. When they tasked Chicago agency OKRP (now BarkleyOKRP) with reinvigorating the brand, they came up with *You Rule*. Have it Your Way → You Rule is genius in that it builds upon Burger King's well-established legacy they have spent decades building, while retargeting their core consumer: A younger generation that believes more strongly than ever in self-empowerment. That's a soulful brand offering meaning to their consumers.

In my experience, the tagline is some of the most challenging and most fun work the copywriter might ever have. Because of all of the work you've done on the verbal identity so far, the ideas often come quickly. But take your time. Like a name, many of the ideas you like at first, you'll hate after a few days of letting them breathe. (That being said, don't discount the early, lighting-strike ideas. They are some of the best.)

The Client Presentation

There is nothing more terrifying and exhilarating than presenting the client with their brand's identity. They have everything on the line. As do you.

But don't be spooked. One of the most important criteria for success in presenting is to enjoy yourself. Remember that we are building soulful brands. As the bestower of life to the brand, it should be presented with anticipation, energy, and joy. And always like a preacher: with clarity and conviction.

It cannot be emphasized enough to practice each presentation multiple times. You need to know the material backward and forward but, more importantly, you want to be so familiar with it that you can focus on how you present it. You don't want to fill space with "ums" and "ers" or trip over words. Practice out loud. Make edits to anything that causes you to stumble. The more prepared you are, the more relaxed and confident you will be. And confidence can sell just about anything. In fact, the client will be looking to you to give them confidence that this is the way to go.

> **"**
>
> **As the bestower of life to the brand, it should be presented with anticipation, energy, and joy.**

I recommend splitting up the verbal identity into three different presentations in the following way:

First presentation: Naming

Because of its importance and the personal, subjective nature of brand naming, it deserves a presentation of its own. It doesn't need to be a large or long presentation. I usually present three slides per name.

- **Slide 1**
    - The context of the name candidate—its category (or bucket)
    - Why the category is appropriate
    - Three to four bullets that will support the name, taken from the positioning, brand promise, and/or USPs
- **Slide 2**
    - The name candidate, along with a supporting photo/image

- **Slide 3**
  - Three to four bullets explaining why the name works (reinforcing the bullets from slide 2, with additional selling points)

Your job when presenting names is to sell each one of them as an exciting, viable candidate. That being said, don't sell too hard. As discussed in the naming chapter, any good name shouldn't need a ton of explanation or hype. It should, for the most part, sell itself. Try not to show preference for any of the names, unless the client asks for your opinion. This is common, so be prepared with the names you feel passionate about, and why you think those names are such a great fit for the brand.

Second presentation

- Positioning
- Brand Promise
- Mission/Vision
- Brand Values
- Brand Narrative
- Brand Persona & Tone of Voice

In this presentation, you are revealing the soul of your brand. All of these elements build on each other to give the client a comprehensive understanding of how their brand will be understood on its most meaningful level. When we've done our job well, these are the elements that create the ability to attach to the subconscious of our audiences. Therefore, it's important to deliver this presentation in a way that feels natural. It should have an easy flow, without too many stoppages. While I find it very helpful to point out certain words, phrases, or details as I go along, I try to do it quickly. You want the client to feel the rhythm of this part of the identity so that they can quickly understand how it all works together. I recommend ending the presentation with one slide that groups all of these elements together.

As for each slide in the presentation, I haven't found any hard and fast rules other than to keep each slide digestible (not too much content), and use the walk-up method when appropriate. For example, in the narrative, maybe reveal one paragraph at a time. Or for the values, reveal one at a time. This is so the client doesn't read ahead and tune you out while you're still on the first part of the slide.

Third presentation

- Audiences
- Competitive Analysis
- Unique Selling Propositions
- Headlines
- Tagline (alongside the Name)

The job of this presentation is to reinforce every preceding part of the verbal brand identity. It might be the least exciting of the three presentations, but it's important because it provides proof of everything else. I recommend formatting each slide with the brand name, position, and brand promise at the top so that the client can have those core elements at the top of their mind when evaluating the content of the slides, and so that you can use them to reinforce your ideas. The tagline comes last, like the final chapter in a great novel.

How you deliver the presentation matters. Make no mistake, you are selling your work. And you are selling yourself. Here are ten tips:

1. Try everything in your power to deliver the presentation in person. If that's not possible, dress as if you are visiting their office.

2. Take your time. Every word matters, so give every word the attention it deserves.

3. Guide the client through the presentation. In the beginning of each section, tell them what they should be looking for. For example, before naming, tell them to pay attention to how each name should satisfy the brand's purpose, value, and/or personality.

4. Assign yourself a couple of bullet points that you want to touch on for each slide, such as overarching themes for each slide that you want to reinforce. Practice where you want to say them during your pitch. It's usually most

effective at the start of each slide or at the end before moving to the next slide.

5. If you are presenting in person, stand up to deliver the presentation, unless physically impossible or for whatever reason, the room just doesn't facilitate it.

6. Don't wave your hands a lot. It's distracting and gives the impression that you are not fully confident in what you are presenting.

7. Do point to things you really want to drive home.

8. Don't stop to ask, "Any questions so far?" This will either lead to an uncomfortable silence, or the client will look for a reason to object to something. It will throw off the entire cadence, and it gives the impression that they should have questions... implying that you are not 100 percent confident in what you are delivering. If the client has a pressing question, they will interject.

"

Make no mistake, you are selling your work. And you are selling yourself.

9. Do ask for any initial thoughts after the presentation. If they are really positive thoughts, it gives you the opportunity to reinforce your ideas. If they are negative, it's an opportunity to counteract and quell their fears before they all get into a room and start group-thinking.

10. At the end of the presentation, tell them that they will want to spend some time with it, at least several days, as the best ideas get even better as they simmer. Plant the seed.

The client presentation is a thrill. Enjoy it, and don't dread it. You have worked really hard to get to this point, and you are prepared. You should be so well-versed in what you are presenting at this point that you can focus on simply telling a story. In fact, you should look at it as if you are giving the client a great gift. If the client requests a few small changes here and there, it is not a failure. It is confirmation that you have created a brand worth investing energy into. It will only get better now that the client is fully invested in its success. If it bombs, draw their attention to the process. Let them know that the building blocks are all in the right place and that you just need to reorient. Ask for another meeting as soon as possible to find the point of failure. Then get back to work and turn around revisions as quickly as you can.

But this won't happen.

I've been using this method to build soulful, meaningful brand identities for fifteen years, and I've never bombed one completely. You won't, either.

Good luck. Have fun. And please let me know how it's going or how it went. I'm happy to chat anytime.